FICTION

WRITERS' PHRASE BOOK

Essential Reference and Thesaurus

for Authors of Action, Fantasy, Horror, and Science Fiction

JACKSON DEAN

CHASE

www.JacksonDeanChase.com

— For those who know the agony of writer's block. —

First Printing, May 2016

ISBN-13: 978-1533064547

ISBN-10: 1533064547

Published by Jackson Dean Chase, Inc.

Printed by CreateSpace

FICTION WRITERS' PHRASE BOOK

PUBLISHER'S NOTES

Want FREE books? Visit the Author at:
www.JacksonDeanChase.com

WARNING:

Do not read this book unless you are ready to beat writer's block forever!

CONTENTS

PART 1: DEATH and DYING

BLADES

BLUDGEONS

BURNING

FUTURISTIC WEAPONS

GUNS

PART 2: HUMAN SUFFERING

PART 3: MAN AGAINST NATURE

ELEMENTAL FURY

WILDLIFE

PART 4: WORDS of POWER

HELL'S COLORING BOOK (Thesaurus)

ACTION VOCABULARY (Thesaurus)

PREFACE

Are you suffering from writer's block? *What if I told you this book could help solve your problem in just a few pages?* I know that's a big promise, but I wouldn't be making it if I didn't believe it was true. In fact, I believe it's impossible for you to flip through this book and *not* be inspired. And that's the thing—my descriptions are not supposed to replace your creativity. They're designed to *inspire* it!

THE GOAL OF THIS BOOK

Feel free to mix-and-match my descriptions or make up your own. You also have my permission to use them "as is," but my goal is not to churn out more writers who sound just like me. My goal is to help you hone your voice as an author, to help you be the best YOU you can be.

This book is a sampler for the rest of my *Writers' Phrase Books* series. There is **no new content**, but some may be new to you if don't own them all. I've included brief sample descriptions for writing action, animals, emotions, and weather, plus two special time-saving thesauri for colors and combat (mundane, magical, and psychic). I've also added a few of the writing exercises and advice sidebars from the other books to help you out. Ready to beat writer's block? Let's get started!

Jackson Dean Chase

www.JacksonDeanChase.com

P.S.: All the books in the *Writers' Phrase Books* series are intended as stand-alone volumes, so there's a fair amount of overlap between them. Unless you regularly write in different genres or create cross-genre mash-ups, you probably only need to own the *Phrase Book* that best fits your genre. And if you're looking for more help than just writing descriptions, check out my other #1 best selling author advice books: *How to Start Your Novel*, *How to Write Realistic Characters*, and *How to Write Realistic Men*.

INTRODUCTION

I'm going to tell you a secret: *A lot of what you write isn't what you say, it's how you say it.* Sure, characters, story structure, and dialogue are important. There are a ton of books written on those subjects for a reason. But you could be an expert in all those things and still fail to tell a compelling story.

Why? Well, to be a truly great writer, you must constantly find new ways to say the same old things. Let's say you're writing a novel about a a ninja assassin. How many different ways can you think of to describe silently killing a man? Or how that feels? What about describing the weather, the wildlife? Remember, these things are going to come up dozens of times and you've got hundreds of pages to fill!

It doesn't matter if you're writing the next *Jack Reacher*, *Star Wars*, or *Game of Thrones*. The same problem applies. Sooner or later, you'll find yourself writing the same descriptions over and over. And you'll agonize over each and every one, wondering how to inject new energy into them. But what if you didn't have to? What if you had an entire book of ready-made tags to inspire you at a moment's notice?

TAG—YOU'RE IT!

Wait! What are tags, you ask? Tags are short descriptive phrases peppered between the dialogue and strung throughout the narrative. Done with skill, the reader never notices them, but their dramatic resonance is deeply felt.

Consider the difference between saying, "He glared at her and she became afraid," or "His gaze burned with such intensity she felt her soul shiver." Which do you prefer? Which is more exciting? Sure, both get the author's point across, but the second is more likely to leave the reader breathless and scrambling to turn the page.

Tags are like bullets. They are the greatest weapons in a writer's arsenal. The more you have, the more firepower you can bring to bear, blasting boring lines to bits and breathing new life into even the most mundane characters and situations.

INSTANTLY WRITE BETTER FICTION

This book provides the tools you need to get the job done for those writing within the Action, Fantasy, Horror, and Sci-Fi genres.

Regardless of genre, every story requires building the right atmosphere to create an emotional connection to its reader. Without one, why would anyone care if tough guy Snake Samson gets trapped in the secret base of the terrorist commandos? He'd just be human hamburger like so many cardboard characters in bad novels and B-movies. But if you can get inside Snake's head and really *feel* what it's like to be him, you can make the reader love him, fear for him, and pray he survives the fight.

In the best fiction, whether you make Snake a "throwaway" victim in the prologue or the hero himself, he becomes a stand-in for readers to project themselves into and identify with. Readers *want* to feel his fear, his isolation, the sense of impending doom hanging over him as all hope seems lost. That is what turns what might have been a cheap action scene into a moment of grueling suspense.

So how do we make our example character more meaningful? We assign Snake's thoughts, words, and actions greater power with every tap of our keyboard. In short, we punch him up with tags. And we do the same for the terrorists. And everyone else who matters.

Use your intuition. Not every line needs to be punched-up. After all, sometimes it's perfectly fine (and perhaps even *more* dramatic in a minimalist sense) to say, "He shot him," instead of "The bullet blazed through bone, spattering brains in a crimson mist."

Nor is it wise for every act, thought or description to be over-the-top or made to stick out unnecessarily. But when you want to really emphasize something, to build atmosphere and heighten emotion, nothing beats a well-written tag.

HOW DO I USE THIS BOOK?

At the very least, just flipping through these pages should jumpstart your creative juices, especially if you've come down with a bad case of writer's block. You can use the tags as writing prompts to help you generate new scenes or even entire stories, but the most common method is to use them as quick "fill in the blanks" whenever you need a line. You have my permission to copy them "as is," or customize them however you like.

Some tags are more specific than others, so you may find it helpful to swap out whatever doesn't work for you with whatever you need. For example, changing the gender of the character or type of weapon and/or action is easily done, as is replacing the generic pronouns given with your character's names or some other vivid description instead (e.g., changing "the man" to "the cruel killer").

You can achieve a variety of exciting effects by mixing and matching tags (or parts of tags) from the same or different categories to create new ones. Say you need to describe Snake seeing a tiger for the first time and your mind draws a blank. Simply flip to the "Man Against Nature" section, then to "Animals." Scan the listed tags until you find one you like, then use it "as is," combine it with others to come up with completely new ones.

For example, you could combine "The tiger was a flashing nightmare of black and orange," and "The lion unsheathed its killing claws," to become "The tiger was a nightmare of killing claws."

So you not only have all the individual tags as written, but you also have an incredible number of combinations—a number limited only by your imagination. There's no wrong way to use this book except not to use it. *It's yours.* Feel free to tinker with it. Mark it up, write in the margins, but whatever you do, have fun!

Jackson Dean Chase

www.JacksonDeanChase.com

– HOW TO EXTERMINATE WEAK WRITING –

Here are three easy exercises designed to seek and destroy slothful descriptions. Pick a category or subcategory of tags that you know will be important to your story, especially a subject you feel you're weak on (such as "Wildlife" if you're writing a jungle adventure).

Exercise #1: Read all the listed tags from your category or subcategory, making note of the top ten tags you like and the bottom ten you don't. Now challenge yourself to revise, combine, or otherwise alter all ten of your favorite tags, then do the same to improve your least favorite ones.

Exercise #2: Combine parts of tags from one category with those from another, mixing-and-matching as best you can to create new effects. For example, a specific headshot from "Guns" could be combined with a kill from "Decapitation and Head Trauma." You could take this one step further, using an entirely different weapon (such as an axe), or maybe even making the head explode or be torn off by a monster or magic spell.

Exercise #3: Challenge yourself to come up with at least ten totally original tags on your favorite subject. Dig deep, and feel the gates of inspiration open!

— PART 1 —

Death and Dying

Well-written scenes of violent conflict (and its aftermath) are a critical component of many genres, from fantasy to horror and beyond. The following section will jump-start your combat, gore, and dead body discovery scenes.

— BLADES —

Axes, Hatchets, and Cleavers

1. The axe cleaved, death riding in its wake

2. The axe made a red ruin of his chest

3. The axe chopped down with hellish fury

4. The deadly axe crunched home

5. The big blade buried itself in his skull

6. He hurled the axe, desperate to strike

7. The honed hatchet flew from his fist

8. The hurled hatchet bit through bone, crushing ribs

9. Meat cleaver raised high, the killer charged

10. The cleaver chopped through his chest

Broken Glass

1. The broken bottle was better than no weapon at all

2. The broken bottle raked out

3. The broken bottle caught her throat

4. The emerald bottle slashed deep

5. The broken bottle turned his face into a crimson mask

6. She used the broken bottle to ward the men off

7. He smashed the bottle, making it into a makeshift blade

8. The glass drew a savage red line across her pale throat

9. Glittering shards rained from the broken skylight

10. The stained glass exploded in a rainbow of death

Chainsaws

1. The chainsaw shaved off his head

2. He dragged the chainsaw across her neck and laughed

3. Gushing red, the chainsawed corpse toppled to the barn floor

4. He swung the smoking machine into her path and revved it

5. The buzzing blade savaged her soft, white throat

Knives, Machetes, and Swords

1. The hunting knife whispered from its sheath

2. He took an electric carving knife to her screaming face

3. He thumbed the switchblade's trigger

4. The dagger slid between bloodied ribs, seeking vital organs

5. The machete slashed though the arm as easily as hacking brush

6. The sword sliced down, ending his screams

7. His blade tore the enemy open in a fountain of flashing red

8. The blade sprang free from its scabbard

9. The blade felt good in his hand, as did the deaths that followed

10. The sword swung in savage fury

Razors and Scalpels

1. The razor had done its work

2. The razor ripped across her neck

3. Glittering death flashed from the surgeon's blade

4. A scalpel in his hand, the mad doctor prescribed death

5. The scalpel slid easily into her soft flesh

— BLUDGEONS —

Brawling and Martial Arts

1. He hit hard and strong

2. He hit fast and fierce

3. He backhanded her across the face

4. He rained down a flurry of blows

5. He landed a lucky blow

6. Her red nails raked his cheek, clawing for the eyes

7. He knocked the guy out with a good right to the jaw

8. He circled his opponent like a shark smelling blood

9. Hairy knuckles crashed home, knocking her senseless

10. Punch after punch, the big man fought on

Crushing Weapons and Objects

1. The hammer caved in his skull

2. The sledgehammer pounded his skull into grisly paste

3. The baseball bat hit a bloody home run across his face

4. The bat hit a grand slam upside his head

5. The brass knuckles beat him bloody

6. The 2x4 cracked against his jaw, shattering it

7. The nightstick left a bloody knot on his head

8. The crowbar crunched down with blinding force

9. The pavement took him in a red asphalt embrace

10. The body burst on impact, splattering the pavement hot red

Mechanized Death

1. The hellish machine ground him to hamburger

2. The gears ground him down, then out

3. What the machine spit out resembled nothing human

4. The old woman rode over the windshield, frail as match sticks

5. The car hit fast, but death came slow

6. A madman sat behind the wheel, his brain humming death

7. He fought the skid, losing control as the car drifted wide

8. The big rig's wheels dragged him under

9. The child became a bloody smear across my windshield

10. The bumper took him low and hard, rolling him over the hood

— BURNING —

Burned Alive

1. The gas-soaked man went up in flames

2. Flame-blackened, the smoking killer lumbered forward

3. Her body was ash that crumbled at my touch

4. They were burned beyond recognition, yet somehow lived on

5. The flames consumed him utterly and not a moment too soon

6. A flaming scarecrow staggered from the wreckage

7. A human comet streaked from the blaze

8. The hungry flames devoured him

9. Burning doom and blasting ruin, the flames crept closer

10. All around us, the ghastly inferno raged

Electrocution (including Stun Guns, Tasers, etc.)

1. The cattle prod shocked and seared her flesh

2. I pressed the stun gun into his side and thumbed the trigger

3. The stun gun shocked him senseless

4. Every muscle contracted against her will

5. Every muscle screamed

Explosives

1. His fist squeezed the plastic explosive into a deadly ball

2. He pulled the pin, counted five, and threw

3. He lobbed the grenade down the hallway

4. The grenade sailed into the crowd

5. The chopper shot twin messengers of death at the target

6. With a deadly *whoosh*, the helicopter launched its missiles

7. The massive blast shook the building

8. The explosion rained crimson hellfire

9. The blast singed his face

10. The shock wave blew over him

Flamethrowers

1. A tongue of fire shot from the flamethrower's barrel

2. The flamethrower spat and streamed liquid fire into the bunker

3. The flamethrower's barrel spilled liquid death

4. The flamethrower hosed them with orange fire

5. The flamethrower's tongue licked the room clean

— Futuristic Weapons —

Drones

1. The drone crashed through the window and exploded

2. The drone's rotors chopped through his hands into his face

3. The drone hovered overhead, reporting back to its master

4. The drone fired its guns in a sustained burst

5. The damaged drone crashed to the earth

Electrified (also see Electrocution)

1. The slaver's stun gloves caught her in their electrified grip

2. He reached out with his stun gauntlets to subdue the prisoner

3. The robo-spear's silver tip crackled with energy

4. The stun-staff knocked him down—and out

5. The cop's stun baton rendered the criminal senseless

Energy (also see Guns)

1. Orange bolts cut the air *(substitute laser color of your choice)*

2. I slapped in a fresh battery pack to reload

3. Energy bolts cut through the darkness

4. The beam bounced off the robot's armor

5. The laser blackened and scorched the tank's armor

6. Lasers lit up the night

7. The steady whine of his laser cut through the noise of the crowd

8. Laser cannons blasted and burned the invaders

9. The plasma bolt punched through the soldier's armor

— GUNS —

Aiming and Firing

1. He aimed with speed and precision

2. The barrel of his gun was a hungry cyclops

3. He sighted on screaming lips

4. He clenched his left eye shut and peered through the scope

5. The scope picked out the details of the target

Ammunition and Loading

1. The trigger clicked on empty

2. The firing chamber clacked open on empty

3. The magazine emptied in under two seconds

4. The firing bolt locked open on an empty chamber

5. The spent shells ejected in a clattering steel rain

Automatic Weapons

1. The full-auto spoke death, and bullets were its words

2. The old man's body jerked with the impact of each shot

3. Flesh and fiber shredded under the Uzi's wicked assault

4. The .30 caliber machine gun chattered blind

5. She shot enough lead to kill three of him and only missed once

6. His gun added to the chorus of death being sung all around him

7. He poured a half-dozen rounds into him for good measure

8. He cut loose with the SMG as soon as the sentry looked his way

9. The SMG chattered until its thirty-round vocabulary was done

Body Hits

1. The first slug tore a hole through his heart

2. The slug struck his rib a glancing blow

3. The bullet drilled him in the spine with a shattering of bone

4. Another slug crashed into his breastbone, throwing him back

5. The fresh round cored out the center of his chest

6. A grapefruit-sized hole punched through his back

7. A trio of holes slammed into his chest

8. The hot lead shower sent the soldier sprawling backward

9. A bullet clipped her thigh

10. The slugs came ripping in at waist level

Gunfights

1. The firefight blazed hot lead through the bitter night

2. The bullets buzzed like angry hornets around his head

3. Men burst from the building with guns blazing

4. He hit the floor in a hail of bullets

5. The renewed gunfire sparked a savage flurry of movement

6. The gunfire halted abruptly

7. A dozen figures cut through the brush, guns blazing

8. A storm of gunfire erupted

9. Shots rang out on both sides, and soon, they were everywhere

10. It was all struggle, all hell—a flashing, blinding, chaos

11. Men scrambled for cover in the sudden chaos

12. Automatic weapons chattered in the distance

Head Shots

1. The soldier's head recoiled from the impact

2. Flesh and brains erupted in a liquid halo

3. A headshot finished the job

4. He lost half his face in a frothing red geyser

5. He ate hot lead as his face exploded

6. The .44 decapitated the first man to come through the door

7. Gushing holes were stitched across his forehead

8. He put a mercy round between her panicked eyes

9. The headshot sent the creep to an early dirt nap

10. Her face disintegrated with one pull of my trigger

Misses

1. Bullets chipped the pavement around him

2. The stray slug took out a jagged section of windshield

3. Armor-piercing rounds punched through their protection

4. Hostile rounds were coming closer

5. The shot went wide as he ran for cover

Muzzle Flashes

1. The weapon's muzzle flashed white-hot in the distance

2. The yellow flash of muzzle blasts were visible forty yards away

3. Return fire flashed at him

4. Yellow fire flashed from the treeline

5. Muzzle flashes illuminated the two gunmen in the doorway

Pistols

1. He used both hands to steady the big .45

2. He triggered a 9mm probe in the night

3. The crack of the pistol put an end to him once and for all

4. He swung the .357 around to find his next target

5. Lunging sideways, the detective clawed for his shoulder holster

Rifles

1. The rifleman tensed, waiting

2. He snapped the rifle up, seeking targets

3. Rifle shots cracked in the distance

4. They held their empty rifles like clubs

5. The riflemen advanced, bayonets at the ready

Silencers

1. The silencer coughed against the pillow

2. He eased the silenced Beretta from its leather holster

3. The silenced pistol blew deadly kisses at her command

4. The silencer whispered once into his ear

5. Twice, the assassin's pistol coughed, and twice, men died

Shotguns

1. His shotgun boomed, blasting the door open

2. The boom-stick belched smoke and fire

3. A sudden lick of flame came from the shotgun

4. His shotgun painted the wall a savage red

— IMPALEMENT —

Bows and Crossbows

1. He drew back the bow and took careful aim

2. Bow in hand, he stalked through the long, dark woods

3. The arrows screamed and the sky grew black with death

4. The crossbow bolt skimmed by, startling him

5. Her shot spiked him to the tree

Spears, Spikes, and Pointy Things

1. He used the spear as leverage to force his opponent back

2. He whittled the long branch into a makeshift spear

3. His savaged body slumped down the spear's shaft

4. The javelin pinned her to the ground

5. He used the rifle like a spear, thrusting the bayonet forward

6. The pitchfork tore into him with a cold steel punch

7. The broken tree branch punched through his lung

8. Gristle hung from the bloody meathook

— WRITING EFFECTIVE ACTION SCENES —

To write effective action, don't go into more detail than you have to, and don't let your characters pause to reflect on what is happening. Would you have time to think or say more than a few words in a real fight? No! Short sentences and short paragraphs ratchet up pacing and suspense. Like when our hero confronts gang-bangers:

Snake Samson drew his pistol. The big gun barked, sending a screaming .45 through the closest punk's guts. His body hit the wall in a hot splat of crimson. The remaining gang members panicked. Some ran. Others dove for cover. And the rest opened fire . . .

See how nice and cinematic that reads? It's fast, exciting. *Real.*

— STRANGULATION —

Hanging and Neck Snaps

1. The Hanging Tree's branches were heavy with human fruit

2. The noose tightened around his neck

3. Inhumanly strong hands clutched his neck, twisting, twisting

4. The boy's neck broke like a rotten branch

5. The head flopped forward on its broken neck

Strangling by Rope or Wire

1. He slipped the wire over the guard's head

2. He tightened his muscles to make the wire cut quick and deep

3. The killing wire cut deep, vanishing into his throat

4. The cord wound tightly, pulling him backward into death

5. He yanked back on the rope with savage fury

Strangling by Hands

1. His mouth cried out for air, yet no sound would come

2. His face purpled under the relentless assault

3. His eyes bulged and her tongue swelled, thirsty for air

4. Heavy, crushing hands closed about her neck

5. The hands squeezed until she could breathe no more

6. Her struggles subsided as the air ran out

7. His thumbs dug into her throat, squeezing off the supply of air

8. The air rushed out of him under that ruthless grip

—WOUNDS and CORPSES —

Blood and Gore

1. Choking on his own blood, he staggered back in disbelief

2. Pulsing arteries pumped their last

3. Crimson bubbles burst past gore-caked lips

4. The blood flowed, the children screamed, and the horror began

5. She was wet with gore, glistening in the moonlight

6. He was crowned in crimson

7. He bled out, the stink of copper his only companion

8. Blood flowered from her wound in crimson petals

9. The trail of gore led to a red room washed in death

10. The taste of copper was in his mouth now

Dead Bodies

1. Blood-smeared and shabby, the corpse was clad in old rags

2. The shriveled remains were as forgotten as the victim's name

3. The frozen bodies were stacked like cordwood

4. Worms crawled over her lips like lovers

5. Of the original victims, only the heads remained

6. Their bodies were propped as if in prayer

7. His blood was still, his heart stopped

8. He had died as he had lived

9. A soul-blasted corpse regarded him with unseeing eyes

10. The skeleton leered at her from its hiding place

Decapitation and Head Trauma

1. The man's head disappeared in a red mist

2. Blood and brains burst out of his shattered skull

3. The mad doctor's drill tunneled into her skull

4. The back of his skull burst open like a ripe melon

5. He sputtered and puked as his brains leaked out

6. Melted brain leaked out of the corpse like clumps of gray jam

7. He clutched at the mangled ruins of his face

8. The head tumbled away from the spurting stump

9. He reached for his missing cranium and felt empty air

10. A fountain of red flowed from where his head had been

Dismemberment

1. The air was stained scarlet by his spurting stump

2. The jagged limb jerked, then lay still on the saw mill floor

3. He stared in horror at his severed hand

4. Still twitching, the mutilated member flopped to the floor

5. The killer took his arm off at the shoulder

Eye Injuries

1. His thumbs found the sockets and pressed hard

2. The object pierced her eye before she could even scream

3. His eyes burst like two balloons, weeping black and red

4. The ruined eye dripped to the floor

5. The missing eye rolled under the chair like a child's toy

Gutting

1. Disemboweled, he stumbled back as his entrails spilled out

2. He kneeled in pain, both hands clutching his open abdomen

3. Life drained through that terrible wound, the guts last of all

4. Her guts hung from the rafters like party streamers

5. His guts steamed and writhed like snakes in a sauna

6. The first yellowish loops of intestine squirmed from the wound

7. The blade gutted him like a fish

8. Frantic fingers clutched and clawed at her mutilated belly

9. He collapsed in a crumpled heap of mangled guts and gore

10. The madman strangled the woman with her own intestines

11. As his guts leaked out, he knew this was the end

Whips and Torture

1. The sadistic woman chuckled softly, brandishing her whip

2. The sting of the lash carried the weight of his authority

3. The chains were cold against my skin

4. The handcuffs bit into cruelly into my wrists

5. The iron poker glowed red-hot against his skin

6. Teeth were pried out amid the crunching of bone

7. The toothless maw gaped at me, a blood-drooling mess

8. The needle pinched, injecting agony

9. Nailed to the cross, her expression was anything but angelic

10. The torturer's gaze was hollow, his eyes cruel and dead

11. The blood-mad fiend began his butcher's work

PART 2

Human Suffering

Conveying addiction, emotion, and sickness is a skill every author needs, regardless of genre. Writing the human condition well is how you get readers to empathize with your characters.

— EMOTIONS —

Ambition and Greed

1. He was young and ambitious, with an eye for conquest

2. Her ambition was to control him utterly

3. She had a ruthless, predatory mind

4. Greed was her only lover

5. The only god she bowed to was greed

Fear and Surprise

1. Cold terror gripped her

2. She felt an agony of despair

3. Fear knotted inside her

4. The cold light of fear shone in her eyes

5. A soft gasp of surprise escaped her

Hate and Revenge

1. Her eyes grew hot with hate

2. His eyes bulged with hate

3. Hate came off him in waves

4. The hatred gnawed at him

5. The wrath was upon him

6. It was foolish to confront him in this mood

7. His heart was black with vengeance

8. Hatred burnt her bitter soul black

Jealousy and Lust

1. The cruel worm of jealousy burrowed into her

2. Her jealous nature forbid her from forming close attachments

3. Lust burned in his brain and he could think of nothing else

4. Cold eyes caressed her with lusting, invisible fingers

5. Shame and desire mingled hot in her throat

6. His pulse quickened with forbidden longing

7. A delicious shudder shot through her body

8. His soft words were spoken only in lust, not love

9. Theirs was a mutual attraction, and a mutual destruction

10. What they shared was not love, it was madness

Sadness and Despair

1. Only despair dwelled in the smoking ruins of my soul

2. Hot tears of shame slid down her rose-colored cheeks

3. Blinded by tears, the grieving girl ran from him

4. Sobbing, she begged for forgiveness

5. Tears fell like rain from her troubled eyes

6. Despair twisted and turned inside her

7. The torment of his decision kept him up at night

8. Her heart ached with the loss of her friend

9. Her face was ashen with grief

10. Her voice was thick with sorrow

11. The dismal weather did nothing to warm his spirits

— PROBLEMS —

Alcohol and Drugs

1. The wine numbed her and the pills did the rest
2. The captain was well into his cups by then
3. The liquor smashed all reason from her lips
4. Though his words were slurred, their meaning was clear
5. His steps were slow, his speech slurred
6. The needle's pinch gave sweet relief from the pain of life
7. Senses swimming, she knew she'd been drugged

Disease and Disfigurement

1. Rusty-red blotches marred a once-handsome face
2. I turned away in disgust at what he'd become
3. Her skin was a patchwork horror of burst veins
4. They were pus-filled savages, living lepers
5. A pulpy red paste poured from every orifice

Nausea, Fainting, and Vomiting

1. Reason fled, along with the contents of his stomach
2. She clutched her belly and doubled over
3. Barf-coated lips begged for mercy
4. There was a smell of rot that pierced the senses
5. The bum smelled of the sewer and forgotten dreams
6. The room spun and the floor rose up to meet him

PART 3

Man
Against Nature

Even if you're not writing a wilderness adventure, sooner or later, nature comes into play, whether it's animals, terrain, or weather. This section keeps those scenes interesting.

— Elemental Fury —

Cold and Ice

1. The frost had taken his fingers, but not his pride

2. The frostbitten hands were black and mottled from exposure

3. The blizzard howled, but not so fiercely as the beast he fought

4. Snow-blind, he staggered across the frozen waste

5. The once-pure snow had turned to sickly brown slush

Earth and Stone

1. Wet earth clung to him

2. The open grave gaped wide, ready to receive him

3. With each passing shovelful of earth, the grave widened

4. The weathered stone was old, crumbling

5. The dusty ground was cracked and broken, parched of all life

Heat and Flame

1. It was an arsonist's dream, an image of hell

2. The city burned, a sea of black and orange against the night sky

3. Dying, the fireplace hissed and sputtered

4. The sun glared like an open wound in the sky

5. The desert sands were a vast dune sea

6. The shifting sands swallowed any hope of survival

7. The sun was sinking, taking all hope and warmth with it

8. The volcanic crater smoked and steamed in the dying light

Night and Shadow

1. There was a furtive movement of black on black

2. He moved like one of night's many shadows

3. Darkness clung to him like a shroud

4. The night was alive with the sounds of death

5. Clinging to the darkness, he was careful not to be seen

6. From the shadows, the night whispered secret terrors

7. He moved swiftly through the fog

8. He became one with the darkness

9. The crescent moon clawed the night sky

10. Black clouds hid the moon in a sea of night

Water and Wind

1. Thunder boomed and the sky grew black

2. The storm raged and lightning struck nearer each time

3. The storm was one step ahead of us

4. It was hopeless to evade the gathering storm

5. Storm clouds gathered overhead

6. There was no end to the storm that raged outside

7. The storm's power passed and little by little, the sun came out

8. The storm lashed out at us with all its fury

9. The dismal wind sent a chill up my spine

10. The wind blew through that barren place like a lost child

11. The first gray drops of rain fell on my cheek

— WILDLIFE —

Animals

1. The bear charged, black eyes promising death

2. The tiger was a flashing nightmare of black and orange

3. The lion unsheathed its killing claws

4. The big cat prowled silently

5. Hungry green eyes peered from the panther's skull

6. The wolf loped forward, hungry for the kill

7. The cat's claws dug bloody furrows in my arm

8. The tomcat yowled and screeched

9. The cat watched me with knowing eyes

10. The Doberman growled and padded forward, teeth bared

Bats and Birds

1. Raven wings beat the sky black

2. In a furious flapping of wings, the eagle descended

3. The eagle screamed, a diving mass of claws and feathers

4. With a vicious nod, the falcon's beak pecked out her eye

5. The parrot spoke better English than its master

6. The parrot croaked the killer's name

7. The owl's gold eyes glared down at me

8. The seagulls picked at the ghastly remains in that watery hell

9. Overhead, the bats formed a ceiling of fur and leather

Reptiles

1. The snake struck, twin fangs flashing like knives

2. The cobra swayed up from the temple floor

3. The cobra's hood unfurled

4. The crocodile knifed through the water, silent and deadly

5. The alligator's scaly tail slapped me back in a crushing blow

Vermin

1. Spider webs clung to my hair as I pushed my way forward

2. Lice crawled over her scalp like dandruff from hell

3. Maggots made short work of the corpse

4. The air was black with the buzzing of flies

5. The fly buzzed, regarding me with dull red eyes

6. The defiant rat glared at me with beady red eyes

7. Hungry rats swarmed over the body

8. Rats gnawed his mangled limbs

9. With a terrified squeak, the rat fled

10. Rats poured from the tunnel, desperate to escape

Water Predators (Non-Reptilian)

1. Shark fins circled the survivors

2. The sharks swarmed forward, hungry for the kill

3. The squid's tentacles dragged me closer to its snapping beak

4. The crab's claws dug the meat from his eyes

5. The piranha gathered and gorged on the blood-red feast

— Dangerous Places —

Exotic Locations

1. The cave grew moist with bat droppings

2. Stalactites hung like stone teeth from the cavern ceiling

3. Decay ravaged the ruins like a scavenger in the night

4. The mist-shrouded island was haunted by a sinister past

5. The steaming jungle was a vast green inferno

Rural Locations

1. The cabin door creaked shut, sealing the four walls of her fate

2. The land was wild, abandoned

3. The villagers here had a strange, inbred look about them

4. These villagers were a dull, sullen lot

5. Even the trees seemed tainted

Urban Locations

1. A smoky haze hung over the city

2. Despair and decay clung to the neighborhood

3. All hope crumbled behind those gray walls

4. The alley was thick with shadow

5. The streets were choked with corpses

6. Flaming cars blocked our path

7. Crows flew overhead, but of people, we saw no sign

8. Walking those darkened streets, I felt terribly alone

— PART 4 —

Words of Power

There are a lot of different ways to say the same thing, and it's hard to keep track of them all! This section serves up a handy time-saving thesaurus to help you quickly and easily find the right words to describe colors and combat actions (including magic and psychic abilities).

— HELL'S COLORING BOOK —

By mixing colors with other words and/or doubling-up similar shades, you can quickly come up with powerful descriptions, such as "the October sky was ghoul-gray" or "the starless night was steeped in shadow."

Black

Anthracite, black pearl, blue-black, coal, crow, dark, dead, ebony, ink, jet, midnight, moonless, night, obsidian, onyx, pitch, raven, sable, shadow, starless, Stygian, subterranean, tenebrous, void, unlit

Blue

Air Force, azure, baby, cerulean, cobalt, cornflower, electric blue, delft, federal, ice, indigo, lapis lazuli, marine, midnight blue, navy, neon, ocean, peacock, periwinkle, powder, Prussian, robin's egg, royal, sapphire, sea-blue, sky, slate blue, sorrowful, steel, teal, turquoise, ultramarine, wedgewood

Brown/Beige

Bay, brick, bronze, brunette, buckskin, café au lait, caramel, chestnut, chocolate, cinnamon, cocoa, coffee, copper, drab, dun, earth, ecru, fawn, foxy, ginger, hazel, henna, khaki, mahogany, maple, mocha, mud, mushroom, nut brown, nutmeg, pecan, raisin, roan, rosewood, saddle, sepia, tan, tanned, taupe, tawny, toffee, tortoise shell, umber, walnut

Gray

Ashen, bleak, charcoal, cloudy, dismal, dove, drab, dreary, dull, gloomy, grizzled, gunmetal, hoary, iron, murky, overcast, pearl, sickly, silver, slate gray, smoky, sooty, somber, stone, sunless, tattletale, tombstone

Green

Aqua, aquamarine, bluish-green, celadon, chartreuse, emerald, envy, forest, grassy, hunter, jade, jealous, kelly, leaf, lime, malachite, mist, mold, moss, olive, pea, pine, sea-green, verdant

Orange

Amber-orange, apricot, atomic tangerine, bittersweet, burnt orange, carrot, champagne, coral, deep carrot, flame, lion, orange peel, orange-red, peach, pumpkin, safety orange, sunset, tangelo, tangerine

Purple

Açai, amaranth, amethyst, aubergine, azurite, blackberry, bluebell, crocus, eggplant, electric purple, frostbite, fuchsia, heliotrope, hibiscus, imperial, indigo, lavender, lilac, lotus, magenta, mauve, orchid, pinot noir, plum, psychedelic, royal, thistle, Tyrian, violet, wisteria

Red/Pink

Apple, auburn, beet, blood, brass, brick, burgundy, candy apple, cardinal, carmine, cerise, cherry, cinnamon, cinnabar, claret, cochineal, crimson, currant, dusky rose, fire, fire engine, fulvous, garnet, hellish, lobster, maroon, ox-blood, raspberry, red amber, rose, rosy, rubescent, rubicund, ruddy, ruby, russet, rust, salmon, sanguine, scarlet, shrimp, strawberry, terra cotta, Titian, Tyrian, tomato, vermeil, vermilion, wine

White/Off-White

Alabaster, anemic, bleached, bloodless, chalk, colorless, cream, deathly, drained, drawn, ecru, eggshell, ghostly, ivory, lily, magnolia, milky, milky quartz, moon, moonstone, oatmeal, opal, oyster, pale, pallid, parchment, pasty, peaked, pinched, salt-and-pepper, snow, vanilla, virgin, wan, washed out, waxen, white jade

Yellow/Gold

Amber, ash blonde, blonde, brass, burnished, buff, cadmium, daffodil, flaxen, fool's gold, fulvous, golden, honey, lemon, jaundiced, jonquil, mustard, palomino, platinum, primrose, sallow, sandy, silver-blonde, straw, tawny, wheat, white-gold

— COLORS WRITING EXERCISE —

Experiment with your own word/color combinations and use them in a descriptive tag. Come up with at least five for each color and feel free to mix-and-match colors (e.g., yellow and brown could be combined as "Her *wheat*-colored hair fell in waves over slim, *tanned* shoulders").

— ACTION VOCABULARY —

Acid and Drowning

Bubble, blister, boil, burn, consume, corrode, crumble, dissolve, disintegrate, decay, eat away/into, erode, gush, immerse, inhale, liquify, scald, sear, sizzle, slosh, slop, soak, spill, splash, spurt, submerge

Attack

Abuse, annihilate, assail, assault, attack, besiege, break through, bull rush, charge, conquer, counterattack, cripple, damage, destabilize, destroy, devastate, disable, fall upon, fire, force, glance, graze, harm, hit, hurt, impair, incapacitate, inflict, injure, lame, lay into, lay waste, maim, mar, overcome, overwhelm, pounce on, raze, ruin, rush, sabotage, savage, scatter, set upon, spoil, storm, strike, swoop, traumatize, triumph over, trounce, vanquish, weaken, wound

Biting and Blood-Drinking

Ate, bit, bite, bolt down, breakfast, chew, chomp, chow down, chug, consume, crunch, demolish, devour, dine, drink, eat, fang, feast, feed, gnaw, gobble, gorge, graze, gulp, guzzle, ingest, lunch, munch, nibble, nip, nosh, partake of, pig out on, polish off, put away, quaff, scarf, sip, snack, snap, swallow, swill, swig, sup, tear, tuck into

Crushing

Bang, bash, batter, beat, belt, bludgeon, bop, brain, break, bruise, bounce, bowl over, bump, burst, bust, butt, clout, clobber, collide, crack, crease, crumple, crunch, crush, cuff, dent, flatten, force, fracture, fragment, grate, grind, hammer, hit, impact, kick, knock, mangle, mash, paste, pound, press, pry, pulp, pulverize, pummel, punch, ram, sap, seize, shatter, slam, slap, smash, smack, smite, snap, sock, splinter, squash, squeeze, strike, stun, thump, trample, wallop, whack, wrench

Cutting and Clawing

Bleed, butcher, carve, chop, claw, cleave, clip, crop, cube, cut, cut to pieces/to ribbons, dice, gash, graze, gut, knife, lacerate, mince, mow, mutilate, nick, pincer, rake, rend, rip, saw, scrape, scratch, score, shred, slash, slice, slit, sliver, snip, split, strip, talon, tatter, tear, trim, whittle

Defense

Bar, barricade, beat back, block, bolster, counteract, curb, defend, disallow, disarm, dodge, drive back, end, evade, exclude, fend off, fight off, force back, foil, forbid, forestall, fortify, guard, hamper, halt, hold off, impede, inhibit, interrupt, keep at bay, obstruct, parry, preclude, preempt, prevent, prohibit, proscribe, protect, push back, repel, repulse, resist, restrain, secure, shield, stave off, stop, thwart, ward off

Fire, Electrocution, Energy, and Explosions

Ablaze, aflame, alight, bake, blacken, blast, blaze, blister, blow up, bomb, bombard, bonfire, brand, broil, burn, burst, candle, careen, char, charge, crackle, detonate, discharge, emit, fire, flame, flare, electrify, electrocute, erupt, explode, fly, fly apart, glow, hum, ignite, incinerate, jolt, juice, launch, let fly, let loose, let off, level, light, lit, open fire, pick off, paralyze, ping, ricochet, roar, roast, rocket, sear, scald, scorch, set off, shell, shock, shoot, shrapnel, singe, sizzle, smoke, smolder, spark, stream, streak, surge, vaporize, up in flames, whistle, whiz, whoosh, zap

Killer and Victim Vocalizations

Babble, bark, bawl, bay, beg, bellow, blubber, blurt out, breathe, burble, cackle, call for help, call out, caterwaul, chant, cheer, choke, chortle, chuckle, cough, cry, cry out, curse, exclaim, exhale, gabble, gag, gargle, gasp, gibber, giggle, grate, groan, growl, grumble, grunt, guffaw, gulp, gurgle, holler, hoot, howl, inhale, intone, invoke, jabber, keen, lament, laugh, mewl, moan, mumble, murmur, mutter, plead, purr, rasp, roar, sing, scream, screech, shout, shriek, shrill, sigh, snap, snarl, snicker, snigger, snivel, sob, squeak, strangle, tee-hee, titter, twitter, wail, weep, wheeze, whimper, whine, whisper, whistle, yell, yelp, yowl

Magical and Psychic Attack and Defense

Abjure, activate, affect, afflict, alter, animate, banish, beguile, billow, blast, block, call forth/up, cascade, cast, change, charge, chant, charm, cloud minds, conjure, counter-spell, course through, curse, deactivate, deceive, delude, demoralize, disappear, drain, emit, empower, enchant, energize, engulf, ensorcel, envelop, evoke, fade, flood, flow, fortify, force, frighten, glamor, hex, hypnotize, induce, inflict, influence, inspire, intimidate, invoke, make afraid, make fearful, mesmerize, numb, overwhelm, panic, petrify, polymorph, pour, prey on, radiate, recharge, repel, repulse, roll over, rush, scare, shape, shield, shock, spook, summon, seethe, shower, spiral, steal, swallow up, swarm, swirl, surge, sway, tear the fabric of space/time, teleport, transform, transmogrify, transmute, twist, undulate, vanish, whirl, writhe

Murder and Execution

Assassinate, butcher, croak, cut down, dispatch, dispose of, do away with, do in, eliminate, end, execute, extinguish, exterminate, finish (off), kill, knock off, murder, massacre, poison, neutralize, polish off, put to death, slaughter, slay, take/end life, terminate

Piercing

Bore through, chisel, feed, finger, force, fork, gouge, gore, harpoon, hole, horn, impale, insert, jab, knife, lance, needle, penetrate, perforate, pierce, pin, pincushion, point, poke, plug, punch, prick, puncture, push, run through, skewer, spear, spike, stab, stick, sting, transfix

Bow/Crossbow: aim, click, crank, draw, fire, fix on, fletch, fly, load, loose, nock, notch, pick off, point, rain, restring, release, reload, train, shower, shoot, sight, snipe, storm, strafe, string, target, trigger, volley

Strangling and Fainting

Asphyxiate, black out, choke, choke out, collapse, conk out, cut off air, cut off breath, dizzy, fall unconscious, gag, gasp, go out like a light, gurgle, faint, fight for air, fight for breath, hang, keel over, knock out, light-headed, loss of consciousness, pass out, seize, smother, stifle, strangle, suffocate, swoon, throttle, unsteady, woozy

Violent Release of Bodily Fluids, Guts, and Organs

Barf, bleed, blob, bloom, blossom, boil, bubble, burst, cascade, deluge, discharge, downpour, drain, dribble, drip, drizzle, drool, drop, dump, eject, emanate, empty, escape, evacuate, excrete, explode, extract, exude, filter, flood, flow, flower, fountain, gag, gargle, geyser, glob, glop, gloop, gob, goop, gurgle, gush, heave, issue, jet, leak, ooze, outflow, outpour, plop, pool, pour, puddle, puke, radiate, rain, ralph, ran, release, remove, retch, river, rush, secrete, seep, shot, slime, sluice, slurp, spill, splash, spat, spatter, spew, splatter, spot, spout, spurt, storm, stream, surge, swam, sweat, tear, torrent, trickle, unleash, unload, upchuck, well out/well up from, void, vomit

Violent Removal of Body Parts and Skin

Amputate, behead, came away/off, carve, chop, cut away/off, decapitate, disembowel, dismember, eviscerate, flay, flew away/off, flog, grab, gut, hack, harvest, hew, lash, lop off, pare, part, peel, pluck, pull, prune, pry, remove, rip, scourge, seize, sever, shave, shear, skin, slice, snatch, snip off, strip away, tear away/off, tug, whip, wrench, yank

ABOUT THE AUTHOR

Jackson Dean Chase brings you Bold Visions of Dark Places. He is the #1 bestselling author of over twenty Young Adult fiction titles and non-fiction books for writers, including *How to Start Your Novel, How to Write Realistic Characters,* and the *Fantasy Writers' Phrase Book.*

Thank you for buying the *Fiction Writers' Phrase Book!*

If you enjoyed this book, please leave an online review. Even if it's just a few lines, your words can make a difference to help reach new readers.

Have a question or suggestion? Or just want to say hi?

Jackson loves to connect with his fans! Friend or follow him online.

Website: JacksonDeanChase.com

Facebook: facebook.com/jacksondeanchase

Tumblr: JacksonDeanChase.tumblr.com

Twitter: @Jackson_D_Chase

Email: jackson@jacksondeanchase.com

Want to know when Jackson's next book is coming out?

Sign up and get **FREE BOOKS** at: **www.JacksonDeanChase.com**

There's NO SPAM, and your email address will never be sold or shared.

Sneak Preview:

Vampires

As he fed, the years tumbled away, restoring the vitality of youth

His fangs traced the delicate hollow of her neck

The coffin creaked and a shriveled, corpse-like hand appeared

Werewolves

Her mouth became a muzzle of yellow fangs and snapping jaws

There was joy in the gnashing of teeth and tearing of flesh

The wolfman glowered at me with slavering jaws and murderous mouth

Zombies

The air was alive with hunger and nothing else

A blood-caked abomination crawled into view, its lower half gone

The cannibal dead cried for blood

Paranormal Romance

His bold red eyes brooked no resistance

Her body ached for his fearsome touch

His kisses were cruel, devouring her will to resist

HORROR
WRITERS' PHRASE BOOK
eBook and Trade Paperback available now

Nuke Writer's Block Forever!

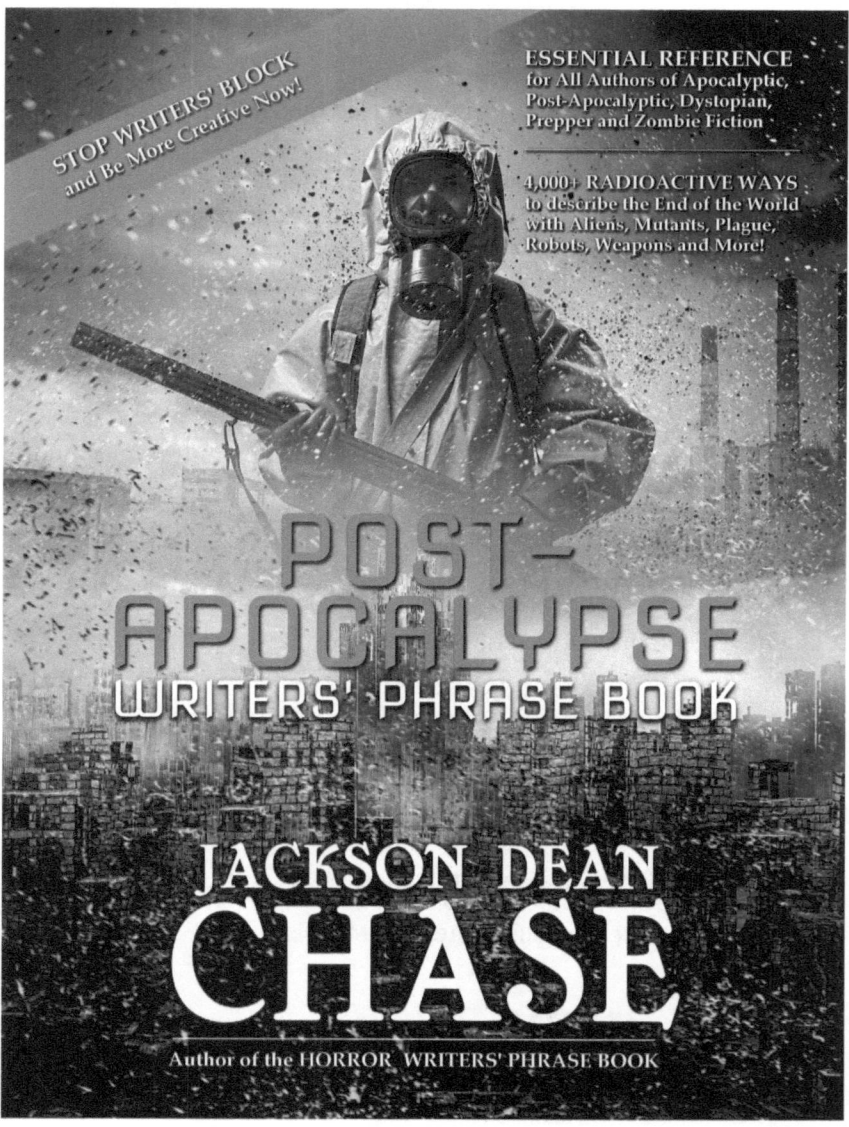

STOP WRITERS' BLOCK
and Be More Creative Now!

ESSENTIAL REFERENCE
for All Authors of Apocalyptic,
Post-Apocalyptic, Dystopian,
Prepper and Zombie Fiction

4,000+ RADIOACTIVE WAYS
to describe the End of the World
with Aliens, Mutants, Plague,
Robots, Weapons and More!

POST-APOCALYPSE
WRITERS' PHRASE BOOK

JACKSON DEAN
CHASE

Author of the HORROR WRITERS' PHRASE BOOK

Writing so hot, it's radioactive! Come along for the ride as #1 bestselling author Jackson Dean Chase takes you deep into the twisted ruins of a new tomorrow. If you write Apocalyptic, Post-Apocalyptic, Dystopian, Prepper, or Zombie fiction, don't to be caught without this book when the bombs drop!

Ruined Cities

The once-proud metropolis still stood as a monument to greed

The bombs had hit hardest here, fusing bodies into the pavement

The city had died as one big traffic jam

Road Warriors

They were pierced and tattooed, the new tribe of this primitive world

The savage men were sharks swimming the long black highway

The leader had a live zombie head as a hood ornament

Nuclear War

Nothing lived under that nightmare sky

Radiation burns were her only makeup now

The mushroom cloud bloomed, a deadly flower on the horizon

Futuristic Weapons

The laser's focusing crystal was damaged and would no longer fire

The drone's rotors chopped into his face

The monomolecular whip sliced through steel as easily as flesh

POST-APOCALYPSE
WRITERS' PHRASE BOOK

eBook and Trade Paperback available now

GET TOUGH ON WRITER'S BLOCK!

Hey, you! Tired of your imagination hitting a brick wall?
Pump up your mental muscles with the *Action Writers' Phrase Book*.
With over 2,000 ways to describe weapons, fights, and more, it's the
perfect workout for authors of Action, Adventure, and Thrillers!

eBook and Trade Paperback available now

SNEAK PREVIEW:

This Time, It's Personal

Her red nails raked his cheek, clawing for his eyes

Hairy knuckles crashed home, knocking her senseless

He circled his opponent like a shark smelling blood

The sword swung in savage fury

The blade felt good in his hand, as did the deaths that followed

Gunfights and Bullet Hits

Flesh and brains erupted in a liquid halo

A dozen figures cut through the brush, guns blazing

The shotgun painted the wall a savage red

Explosions and Fiery Doom

Hellfire roared, bringing damnation and death

Red, yellow, and orange: these were the colors of my hate

A living torch, the man ran to the cliffs and fell to the rocks below

Mechanized Death

A madman sat behind the wheel, his brain humming death

The child became a bloody smear across my windshield

The cars crashed in a grinding shriek

ACTION
WRITERS' PHRASE BOOK

eBook and Trade Paperback available now

NEW BY JACKSON DEAN CHASE

BLAST THROUGH WRITER'S BLOCK!

SCIENCE FICTION

WRITERS' PHRASE BOOK

ESSENTIAL REFERENCE for All Authors of SCI-FI, CYBERPUNK,
DYSTOPIAN, SPACE MARINE, and SPACE FANTASY ADVENTURE

JACKSON DEAN
CHASE

Bestselling Author of *How to Start Your Novel*

Exclusive Sneak Preview:

Aliens

The aliens were wolf-like and savage, covered in shaggy fur

The alien's blue skin shed a soft glimmer under the twin moons

The reptilian soldier rubbed lubricating oil over its scaled skin

The alien was trying to communicate through pheromones, not sound

I felt the gray-faced alien probe my thoughts

The aliens were tall and impossibly thin, possessed of a strange grace

The people of this world were short and squat, perfect for its low gravity

The green-skinned female danced, bending in ways no human could

That these were a primitive, backward people, I had no doubt

Their species were world-bound, unaware of our empire

Planets, Moons, and Asteroids

The atmosphere was gaseous purple, and of land, I saw no sign

Strange mists and fearsome cries filled the jungle night

The loathsome swamp bubbled and oozed

The planet's surface was covered in sentient gray slime

I could only call them trees, but their branches moved like tentacles

This was a water world, but like no ocean I had ever seen

The asteroid's surface was pitted and cracked, covered in minerals

Overhead, the twin moons shone like malevolent eyes in the darkness

A ring of ghost ships orbited the Death Moon

SPACE STATIONS

The station's halls were a uniform white, punctuated by black doors

The station was oddly organic-looking in a way that disturbed me

The station was powered by an interconnected series of alien brains

Getting past the security door required a biometric identi-print

Stern guards blocked my access to the command center

Blast-proof doors came down to seal us in

Red lights flashed in every hall as the self-destruct countdown began

The abandoned station had been built by a long-dead race

BARS AND CANTINAS

The bar smelled of the dashed hopes of a thousand worlds

A motley band took to the cantina's stage

They didn't serve our kind here

Gruff laughter bellowed from the booth near the door

There was no bartender, just some weird kind of fluid dispenser

SPACESHIPS

The gray bulk of the cruiser drifted by

The imperial flagship loomed ahead, weapons locked

The pirate ships were poorly armored but heavy on firepower

The science vessel scanned the planet's surface for signs of life

The battle cruiser locked its tractor beam on us

Ranged Weapons

I set my pistol to "stun" and thumbed the trigger

He slapped a fresh battery pack in my rifle and felt it hum to life

The ship's corridors echoed with the angry whine of blasters

The red beam punched through the enemy's armor

Laser cannons popped down through ports in the ceiling

The drop-down laser cannon swiveled in our direction

A laser grid moved down the hall, slicing through anything it touched

The tangler shot a polymer capsule that quickly expanded into a net

The weird gun fired nano-darts that could reprogram a victim's mind

Melee Weapons

I drew my plasma sword and let it crackle to life

The laser sword lit up the darkened hallway

Powered by my will, the psychic sword blazed blue against the night

The robo-ripper sawed forward, chewing through the soldier's armor

Her monofilament whip cracked, cutting the man in two

The slaver's staff had an electrified tip that stunned its targets

Science Fiction
Writers' Phrase Book
eBook and Trade Paperback coming soon . . .

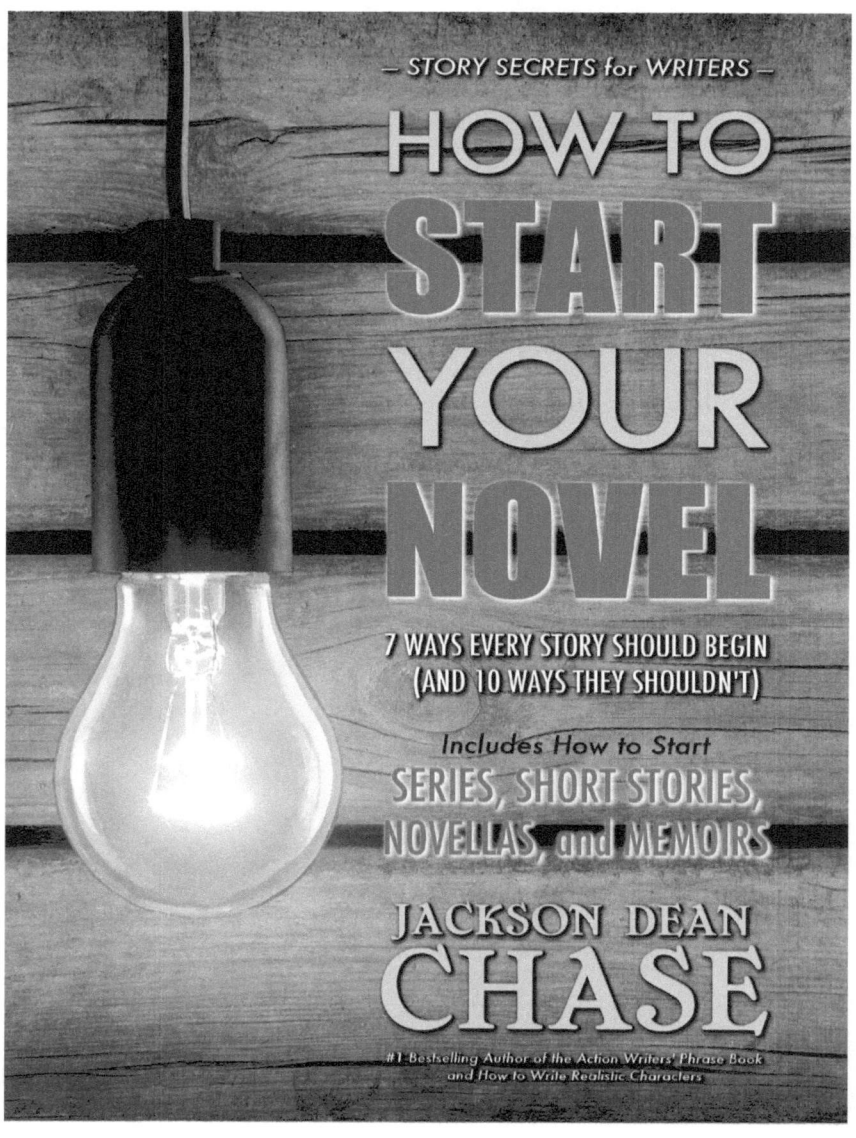

STORY SECRETS for WRITERS

HOW TO START YOUR NOVEL

7 WAYS EVERY STORY SHOULD BEGIN
(AND 10 WAYS THEY SHOULDN'T)

Includes How to Start
SERIES, SHORT STORIES,
NOVELLAS, and MEMOIRS

JACKSON DEAN CHASE

#1 Bestselling Author of the Action Writers' Phrase Book
and How to Write Realistic Characters

The first words on the page are the hardest you'll write. It's easy to get overwhelmed. **How do bestselling authors do it?** That's what I set out to discover. I tore apart my library, scouring the openings to hundreds of novels to see what makes them work and *why*. And do you know what I found? A pattern—**a secret formula** authors use time and time again to deliver **powerful, bestselling results!**

— SNEAK PREVIEW —

HOW TO START YOUR NOVEL

(excerpt from the chapter on starting with dialogue)

Dialogue puts you into the mouth of a character with something brief and important to say. It can't be, "Hello, how are you?" or "Please, sit down." Anything normal is the kiss of death. Dialogue must be powerful and, like action, it must refer to something exciting that either has happened, is happening, or is about to happen, so make sure there is at least a hint of mystery or danger in your words.

> "We should head back," Gared urged as the woods began to grow dark around them. "The wildlings are dead."
>
> —George R. R. Martin, *A Game of Thrones*

We get an immediate sense of peril, and know that there has been a battle, yet some greater danger remains. What is it? We cannot help but find out. Also, notice how the author mentions the darkening forest between the dialogue. That helps set the scene . . . and the danger.

> "Do the dead frighten you?" Ser Waymer Royce asked with just the hint of a smile.
>
> Gared did not rise to the bait. He was an old man, past fifty, and he had seen lordlings come and go. "Dead is dead," he said. "We have no business with the dead."

These next paragraphs introduce another character, Ser Waymer Royce, and create conflict between him and Gared. They also sketch in a few details about the speakers. More importantly, they both keep talking about the dead. By placing such importance on them, we begin to feel uneasy. It's getting dark. The men are in a forest. Night is falling. This is a medieval fantasy world, so it stands to reason there are a lot of superstitions about the dead coming back to life, not to mention ghosts, curses, that sort of thing.

> "Are they dead?" Royce asked softly. "What proof have we?"
>
> "Will saw them," Gared said. "If he says they are dead, that's proof enough for me."
>
> Will had known they would drag him into the quarrel sooner or later. He wished it had been later rather than sooner. "My mother told me that dead men sing no songs," he put in.

The conversation continues, now bringing in a third minor character, Will, who is the hero of this prologue. By saving Will's reveal for last, we get a chance to peer inside his thoughts for a moment before he speaks. This serves two purposes: 1) it breaks up the conversation which helps pacing; and 2) it sheds some light on Will before he ever opens his mouth. By going inside his head and not into the heads of Gared or Royce, we know Will is more important to the story. We establish him as the hero.

Could Will have spoken first? Sure, but sometimes it's better to hold the hero back so he's already been set up by others and the situation clearly established. That frees the hero's introduction from unnecessary clutter.

> "We have a long ride ahead of us," Gared pointed out. "Eight days, maybe nine. And night is falling."
>
> Ser Waymer Royce glanced at the sky with interest. "It does that every day about this time. Are you unmanned by the dark, Gared?"

Danger is again threatened by the mention of night, then dismissed. It's important to have one character who refuses to heed the warning, who is more interested in scoring points via insults or witty remarks. This creates conflict, but it also ramps up suspense.

Note that some questions lead to monologue instead, with the other characters reflecting on their feelings. It's also a valuable opportunity to weave in details that have no place in dialogue:

> Will could see the tightness around Gared's mouth, the barely suppressed anger in his eyes under the thick black hood of his cloak. Gared had spent forty years in the Night's Watch, man and boy, and he was not accustomed to being made light of. Yet it was more than that. Under the wounded pride, Will could sense something else in the older man. You could taste it, a nervous tension that came perilous close to fear.

We need Gared's reaction, but we don't need to jump into his head to get it. By seeing his reaction through Will's eyes, we stress Will's importance. Gared takes on a mentor role, and Royce continues to be the immediate villain. We also get more suspense as Will notices Gared's fear . . .

Want to find out the best ways to begin your story with action, dialogue, mystery, and more? Get the full book now!

HOW TO START YOUR NOVEL

The 7 Ways Every Story Should Begin

(and 10 Ways They Shouldn't)

eBook and Trade Paperback available now